FALLINGWATER

THE MODEL

RIZZOLI
NEW YORK

First Published in the Unites States of America in 2000 by
Rizzoli International Publications, Inc.
300 Park Avenue South, NY 10010

Copyright © 2000
Rizzoli International Publications, Inc.
Text © Paul Bonfilio
Photography © Paul Bonfilio

ISBN 0-8478-2341-5
LC 00-105429

Designed by Bonfilio Design
Printed and bound in Singapore

ACKNOWLEDGEMENTS

This book is dedicated to my father and mother who both served as inspiration to me by their hard work and ability to see a project through to its completion. In particular, my father often assisted me in making special tools to fabricate many aspects of this model as well as aiding me in finding solutions for many problems that occurred during construction of the model. As a teenager and into my adult years, I often observed his ability to make jigs to fabricate complicated metal pieces in his work as a tool and die designer and maker. Much of my creativity and cleverness in building models or in general, the process of solving a problem, is directly attributable to him, and I miss him very much.

Special gratitude is owed my wife Alba and my three girls, Delia, Selena, and Alexis, who put up with my absence while I toiled over this model for a period of two years. Alba was there as well as my dear friends Ted Spagna, Alfred A. Funai Jr., and Athanasios Klidonas, when we spent two days photographing and measuring Fallingwater. Thanks are owed to Edgar Kaufmann, Jr., who provided photostats of Wright's quarter inch scale drawings of the house. These served as the basis for the three eighths of an inch to one-foot scale of the drawings, which served as the basis for the model.

No model, especially of this complexity and dimension, is possible without the aid of other modelmakers and artists. During the years I built models, I had the privilege to meet and work with many fine modelmakers, many of whom often served as the nucleus of a team whenever I built MoMA's models. I learned from them and surely they learned from me. I always credited their names with each of the various models I built and I wish to acknowledge them now, Lenon Kaplan, Larry List, Edith Randel, Norman Baker, Adam Birnbaum, Joseph Zelvin, and George Gabriel.

Of course, my long term relationship and continuing friendship with many of the curators of the Museum has never gone unnoticed. Their cooperation and help has always been a comfort to me. Some have left, but many are still there. I extend my gratitude to Arthur Drexler, Ludwig Glaeser, Stewart Wrede, Matilda McQuade, Robert Coates, Chris Mount, and Terence Riley.

Additional thanks are owed to Lawrence Tallis, Bernard Pismeny, and Lucille Wright, who have assisted me more recently in the latter stages of photographing and writing. Special thanks to my dear friend Ted Spagna, whose photographs appear throughout the book, and who was always there when I needed him. Ted was there when we initially took over 600 photographs of the house and then developed all the film so that the model could be built. Ted died on June 21, 1989. He is sorely missed. And finally, a very special thanks to my daughter Delia, who designed this book; she made the impossible possible.

TABLE OF CONTENTS

FOREWORD

THE ART OF THE MODEL

While much of the language of architecture is arcane to non-professionals, architectural models have an enormous appeal that transcends experience. While they have a specific professional raison d'etre, they are also miniatures – a genre that immediately establishes a very intimate relationship between the viewer and the object.

This intimacy invites a very personal experience as well, the projection of the viewer, through his or her imagination, into a spatial and physical environment that might only exist in the form of the model being viewed.

Another aspect of the broad appeal of architectural models is their craft. In a world that defines most people as consumers, the creation of the architectural model is within a world of making things, of inventing and refining techniques that allow the eye and the mind to enter a world that exists in less than human proportions.

The importance of architectural models is not just in their popular appeal but in their specific function as a tool of the architect. From the time of the ancient Greeks, models have been used by architects to test their own conceptions of form and space, prior to committing their ideas to construction. As such, the art of architecture owes much to the model makers' skill, few of the masterworks which we now revere were not fine tuned and improved though the process of studying their three dimensional characteristics in the form of the model.

If the model has been instructive to architects, it has also proven to be one of the most effective tools in communicating to non-professionals the spatial and physical qualities of a building. In particular, it is hard to imagine what architecture exhibitions might be like without models. The first such exhibition by a museum was held in 1932 at The Museum of Modern Art. Curated by Philip Johnson, the 'International Style' exhibition, as it has come to be known, featured important projects by the leading architects of the day. Each architect had a key project represented by a model. In planning the exhibition Johnson noted the two-fold importance of the models. Firstly, they best communicated to the public the ideas of the architect. Secondly, they were works of art that could become part of the museum's permanent collection. And so they have.

Paul Bonfilio's contribution to the art and craft of model making is considerable. His model of Frank Lloyd Wright's seminal work, Fallingwater, delights and engages the museum's visitors in ways that few other objects at the museum do. Overcoming distance and time, the viewer is able to enter, through Bonfilio's skills, a world of very small spaces and very big ideas.

—TERENCE RILEY

CHIEF CURATOR, ARCHITECTURE AND DESIGN,
MUSEUM OF MODERN ART, NEW YORK

INTRODUCTION

The path to Fallingwater, the model, was indeed a long one, tempered by many years of learning to build architectural models during the course of my studies in architecture at Cooper Union. My experience at Cooper was one that led from cardboard and balsa wood models to acrylic. It was in my fifth and final year when I built a plastic or acrylic model of my thesis house, under the tutelage of John Hejduk, presently the dean of the School of Architecture. I believe that this was the second student-built model in acrylic. Ted Spagna's was probably the first. The use of plastic for a student project, which required machinery such as table saws and drill presses, was an innovation in 1967, when most students were painting cardboard and wood. Nevertheless, these models caught the attention of John Hejduk who then insisted that I build models for him of his various architectural works.

Although these models were crude by today's standards, they had a quality which professor Hejduk liked, and for the next several years I built many of his models in various architectural scales. It was Hejduk's insistence that I build his models that placed me on the road to architectural modelmaking, which lasted nearly twenty years.

My introduction to the Museum of Modern Art (MoMA) was facilitated by another great architect, Richard Meier. Since modelmaking was a part-time endeavor for me, it was difficult to build models for architects who had to meet client deadlines. Also, since I could not compromise on quality, I leaned in the direction of museum models, where there would be sufficient time and more appreciation for detail.

In 1971 I bid for the construction of Villa Stein by Le Corbusier for an upcoming exhibit at MoMA. At first I was told that I was not selected since I was the highest bidder. However, a week later, Ludwig Glaeser, who was then a curator in the Architecture and Design Department, informed me that I was selected at the insistence of Richard Meier, who had seen my models for John Hejduk. Meier had told Glaeser that Bonfilio was the only one who could properly build the Stein model. To this day I am grateful to Richard Meier, because he opened the door which eventually led to the Fallingwater model. It is still nor clear how Meier even knew that I was interested in the Stein model. The museum gave me only three weeks to complete it and I enlisted the help of my father and my old friend, Ted Spagna. The model was painted white, with the use of gray for colored areas of the house. This was done since the museum was unsure of the actual color Le Corbusier used. Later, Arthur Drexler, Director of the Architecture and Design Department, requested my services to repaint the model based on a series of colored axonometric drawings either approved or drawn by Le Corbusier. Meeting Arthur Drexler, a man I initially feared, was to be a pivotal event, which not only led to a respectful friendship but also to the beginning of a long period of museum model making.

During the ensuing years, my friendship with Arthur Drexler solidified into a comfortable professional relationship, which achieved his goal of filling the museum's galleries with architectural models of the great masters and my goal of building them. Arthur had ambitious plans, and many of the models in the permanent collection were built during his tenure. Some of these models included the Barcelona Pavilion by Mies Van der Rohe, the Lovell House by Richard Neutra, and the Glass House by Philip Johnson. There was also a program of repairs and restoration to many of the models in the permanent collection. These included Frank Lloyd Wright's Robie House and Le Corbusier's Villa Savoy and Palace of the Soviets. Prior to his death in 1987, Arthur had planned an ambitious program for models of the "Court Houses" by Mies as well as many other models by the great masters. Unfortunately that part of his dream would not be completed, even though he enabled me to accomplish a large part of my dream.

In the latter part of 1987, I was approached by representatives of Mr. Tom Monaghan, then owner of the Dominos Pizza chain. Mr. Monaghan had distinguished himself as an avid collector of Frank Lloyd Wright furniture and memorabilia. His own headquarters in Ann Arbor, Michigan resembled a Wrightian-designed building. Mr. Monaghan had seen MoMA's model of Fallingwater and decided that he had to have one for his own museum and collection in Michigan. Within months I began construction of a second model of Fallingwater some five years after completing the first one.

1

THE BEGINNING
PHOTOGRAPHS AND DRAWINGS

A COMPLETE PHOTOGRAPHIC RECORD OF THE HOUSE

In order to build the Fallingwater model, it was necessary to fully document the house. Although many books have been written about the house with thousands of photographs available, it was now necessary to photograph the house from the point of view of a modelmaker. Therefore, documenting a single room would require a photograph of each elevation, the stonework in the floor, various three-quarter views, and specific details, such as fireplaces and furniture. In many of the photographs a 12-inch ruler was placed against a wall in order to assist in ascertaining a dimension by scaling it in the photograph. Some of the larger spaces, such as the living room, would require even more photographs. The exterior of the building was

RIGHT: Typical bridge abutment at the railing juncture with a 12-inch ruler for scale.
BELOW: View of Mrs. Kaufmann's bedroom fireplace and varied ceiling heights.

ABOVE: **Bottom view of the boulder beneath the living room hearth.** LEFT: **12-inch ruler alongside the railing at the second floor planter.**

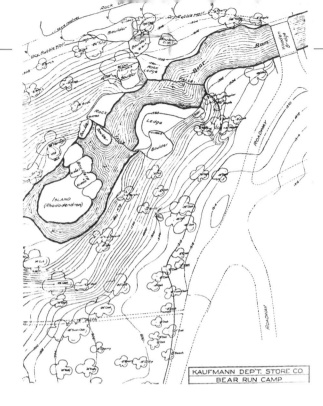

KAUFMANN DEP'T. STORE CO.
BEAR RUN CAMP

OPPOSITE PAGE TOP: **Boulders below the second floor's west terrace.** OPPOSITE PAGE BOTTOM: **Living room view looking west.** LEFT: **Kaufmann survey supplied to Wright.**

also subject to intense photography because of its interaction with nature. Boulders and topography are such recognizable features of Fallingwater that any model must faithfully reproduce them in scale. Indeed, the layers of sandstone beneath the living room, with the cascading waterfall, are as recognizable a form as the house itself. Photographs of the stream, plunge pools, and the waterfall itself would all serve to assist in replicating those patterns of water in the model itself. At least 600 photographs, over a two-day period, were taken of Fallingwater. A representative stone wall was photographed with, again, a 12-inch ruler, which when enlarged to three eights inch to the foot scale, produced a prototypical wall pattern. Innumerable hidden views were photographed to insure that every detail in the house would be reproduced in scale model form. The stone floors, which are always evident in any book on Fallingwater, were photographed with a wide-angle lens to capture most of the room and establish a sense of the pattern.

AN ACCURATE SET OF AS-BUILT DRAWINGS

Edgar Kaufmann Jr. was kind enough to provide the museum and in turn to me, photostats of one-quarter inch-to-the-foot drawings by Frank Lloyd Wright. These drawings were the usual floor plans, elevations, and sections, necessary to understand the house. They were by no means the type of working drawings today's architects would use to construct a building. The drawings had critical dimensions establishing the height of a stone wall or a concrete railing and general dimensions of rooms, but were not laden with dimension lines obscuring the design. Certainly any unknown dimension could usually be determined with an architectural scale. Mr. Kaufmann also provided photostats of details such as the wine kettle in the living room fireplace, the grating, and metal shelves. These were usually at a larger scale of one-inch equals one-foot. The concrete piers, which support the main living-room cantilever, were also shown at a larger scale with a rudimentary indication of steel reinforcements. The collection of these drawings served as the basis for redrawing the house at the larger 3/8-inch scale (by now the norm for models at MoMA). Redrawing the

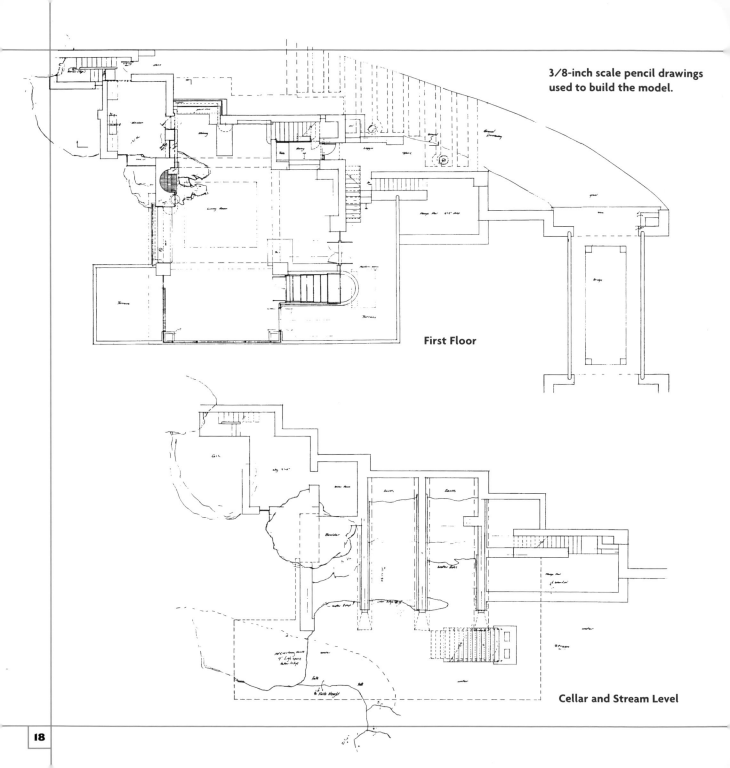

3/8-inch scale pencil drawings
used to build the model.

First Floor

Cellar and Stream Level

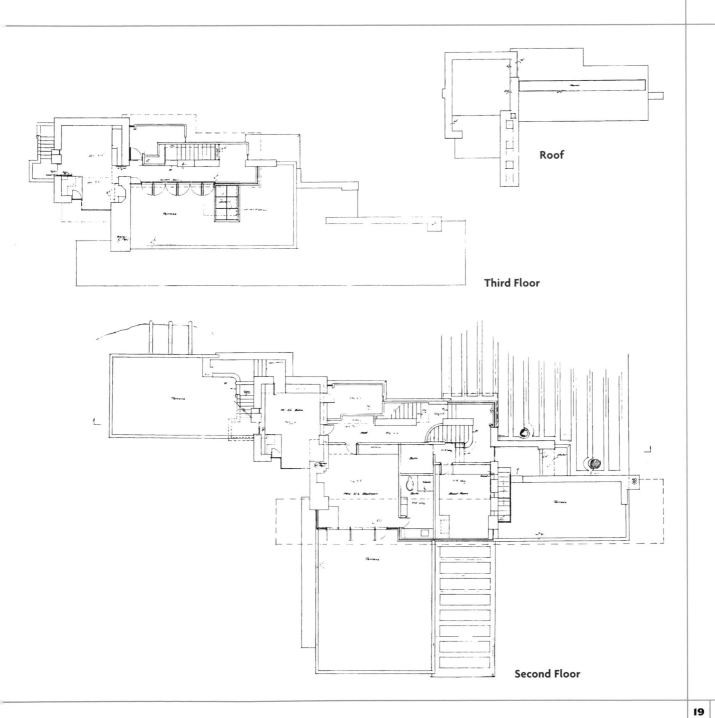

Roof

Third Floor

Second Floor

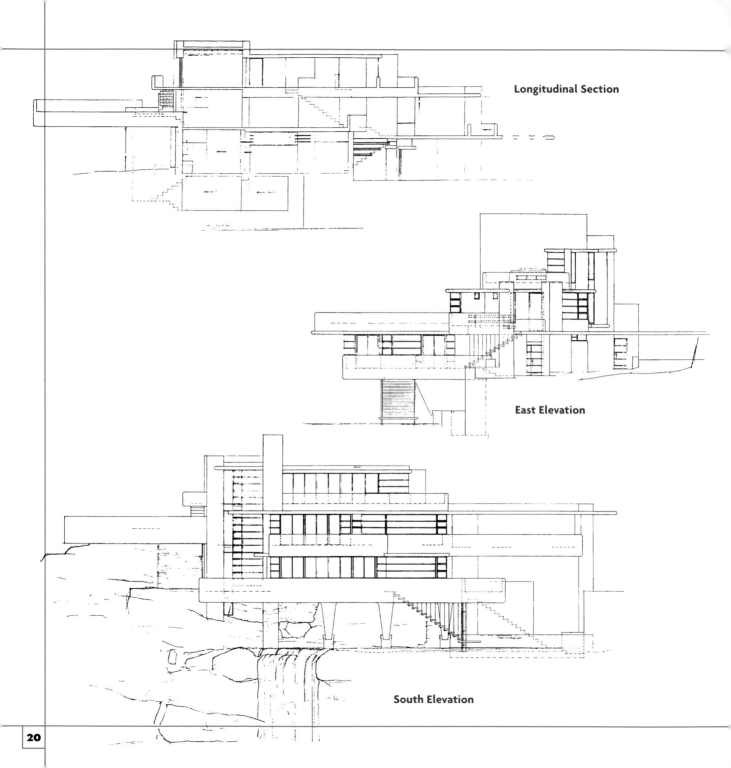

Longitudinal Section

East Elevation

South Elevation

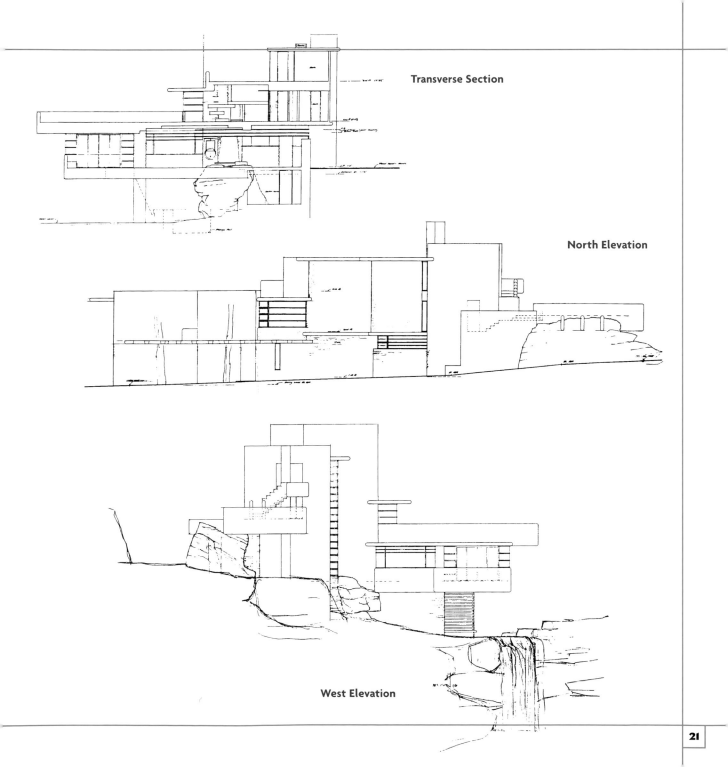

Transverse Section

North Elevation

West Elevation

house, including the cellar level, first, second, and third floors, together with a transverse and longitudinal section and four elevations, would consume three months. However, since the photostats supplied were not fully dimensioned they served as a preliminary set of drawings onto which actual dimensions could be placed during my initial visit and documentation of the house. With these photostats in hand, a tape measure, and the assistance of my wife and three close friends, we proceeded to measure the house. Interior dimensions of every room were taken. Floor to ceiling heights, which varied, were noted. The difference of one inch in the living room ceiling, from the support column to the end of the second floor terrace, was noted. This resulted from a droop of the cantilever of the second floor, which extends beyond the living room below. The position of the topography and boulders was measured against the house and some reference point,

such as the top of a wall. With this information the drawings were begun.

However, as the drawings were completed, an error occurred in the vicinity of the entrance to the house. For some unknown reason, the drawing did not "close". A second visit to the house soon uncovered the cause. I surmised that a correction took place in the field where the road leading to the guesthouse above Fallingwater was widened by one foot. The positioning of a support wall was moved by one foot contrary to the original drawings. Once this correction was made to the 3/8-inch scale drawings, all the drawings soon fell into place and aligned with each other. There were also other minor field changes relating to the heights of stone walls, which were also discovered. Whether they existed or not before, I now possessed an accurate set of as-built drawings from which the model could now be constructed.

The guest house and connecting walkway were also measured, as this was to be a second phase of the model at some later date. However, this portion of the site was never commissioned and therefore the model represents Fallingwater as it was when it was completed in 1937. Regarding the site and topography from which the house grows, the well-known survey supplied to Wright by Edgar Kaufmann provided the context for the cellar-level drawing. This drawing was also at the level of the Bear Run stream and the top of the waterfall. It would later serve as the basis for the four-foot by six-foot base of the model.

THE UNKNOWNS

During the course of my modelmaking career, I learned many construction techniques from fellow modelmakers, as well as developing my own. However, there was always some aspect of a model that was new, and

Composite photograph of the sandstone ledges and the waterfall, a form as recognizable as the house itself.

therefore a new technique had to be developed to render it. In the case of Fallingwater there were many aspects completely unknown to me. Of course I always accepted those unknowns as a challenge, knowing that somehow with enough imagination a solution would present itself. I had never done a waterfall before nor have I ever seen one convincingly rendered. The stonework on the house also presented a challenge but I knew that it was manageable. Other aspects, such as the boulders, windows, and vegetation had solutions from prior models. Nevertheless, Arthur Drexler never knew that I had absolutely no idea how I would build this model. I just knew that it had to be built and was grateful for the privilege of building it.

2

THE BUILDING
EVERY BUILDING HAS A FOUNDATION

LAMINATING FLOOR PLANS TO ACRYLIC SHEETS

With the completion of the floor plans and other drawings showing details and sections, it was possible to convert this two-dimensional reality into a three-dimensional representation. The primary material for the model's construction was acrylic or plastic sheets. This material is either extruded or cast into large four-foot by eight-foot sheets. The material is covered in a thin paper mask, which protects the surface of the acrylic while allowing one to write on it. The problem is how to transfer the layout of the floor plan to the acrylic. One way would be to take advantage of the paper mask and simply redraw the floor plan on it. A better way would be to make a paper print of the respective floor plan and simply laminate it with a rubber cement adhesive to the acrylic sheet. Since each plan was initially drawn over the other and various vertical supports line up, by reproducing each plan in the same medium under the same conditions, the laminated floor plans will also line up. There is always some amount of stretching when a drawing is reproduced in blueprint, black print, or xerox reproduction. Even positive photostats will not perfectly line up with an original. Therefore, once laminated, certain key dimensions should be checked against the original drawings. The acrylic sheets come in various

View of the third floor plan laminated to an acrylic sheet prior to cutting.

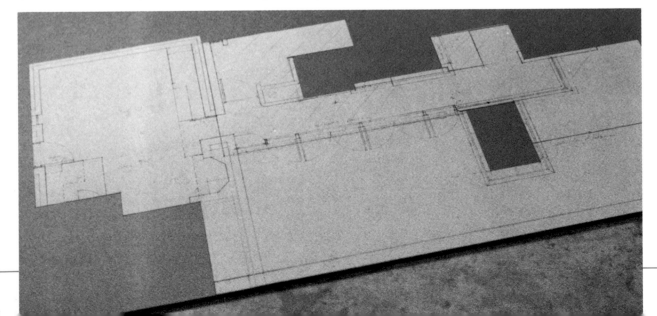

Transferring the floor plan to the acrylic sheet is accomplished by scoring through the paper to the acrylic surface with a sharp metal blade.

thicknesses. In the case of Fallingwater, the section drawings revealed that the slabs of concrete and stone flooring varied in thickness from room to room. The varying thicknesses created different floor to ceiling heights as well as concealing heavy beams necessary for some of the cantilevers. Therefore, the thinnest section acrylic sheet was chosen for the floors that represented in scale the thinnest section of floor slab. In the model, these sheets were 3/16-inch thick. As the floor slab varied in thickness, an additional layer of acrylic, separated by appropriately sized walls, created the varied ceiling system.

CUTTING ACRYLIC SHEETS

After each floor plan was laminated to the acrylic sheet, it was possible to cut the outline of the floor. Plastic is best cut with a table saw utilizing a seven- to ten-inch-diameter, hollow-ground blade. Hollow

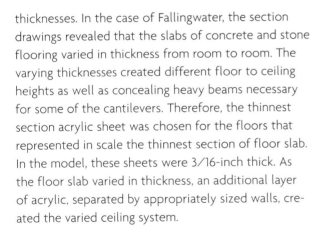

ground simply means that the teeth of the blade are flush to the entire surface of the blade. Hollow ground blades provide a clean cut through the acrylic, unlike a blade for cutting wood, which has alternating bent teeth that tear the acrylic or are unable to cut the sheets at all. Openings within the floor plan area, for example, stairwell openings, were cut utilizing a technique of raising the table saw blade up into the acrylic sheet. By measuring the distance of one edge of the opening to a parallel edge of the floor plan, the table saw fence can be fixed and the blade can be lifted into the acrylic. The corners were hand cut and filed flat. Cutting the floor plans was a very labor-intensive process.

The most difficult aspect of the floors was determining both the outline and depth of the ceilings. Since ceiling heights varied throughout Fallingwater, each floor would have the ceiling of the floor below attached to it. Any beams that were visible or any recessed ceilings, such as in the living room, would be incorporated into the floor above.

Gluing acrylic sheets is accomplished by using solvents, which effectively melt the two surfaces to be joined and create a strong bond. Applying solvents is usually done with a brush or any bottle with a blunt-end needle to flow the solvent into the joint. Capillary action insures that the solvent reaches all surfaces that touch. The Fallingwater model was built on a large slab of marble that provided an absolute flat surface, insuring that when two sheets of acrylic were glued to each other, separated by a series of walls, they would be absolutely parallel to each other. Since Fallingwater has relatively long floor plates, this technique prevented any possible warpage.

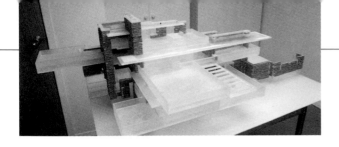

View of each floor of the model in assembly sequence.
FROM TOP TO BOTTOM: **the roof, third floor, second floor,
first floor, and stream level.**

THE USE OF VERTICAL "CORE WALLS"

Fallingwater, structurally, is essentially composed of
concrete floor slabs supported by stone bearing walls.
The "stone walls" in the model were produced with
sheets of "stone" cast in plaster, and an acrylic "core
wall" was used to support each floor. The "core wall"
would have stone-rendered plaster sheets glued to
each side and would provide the support vertically
throughout the model. Utilizing this technique enabled
the model to be completely built in clear acrylic, floor
by floor, with "core walls" glued to each floor representing the centerline of partitions or stone bearing
walls. As each floor is laid one on top of the other,
these core walls would line up vertically, and provide
continuous vertical support.

FASTENING TECHNIQUES

Although the variegated ceilings were interlocking,
much like a puzzle, as each floor was laid on top of
another, it was still necessary to be able to connect
each floor to the one below. The floors of the model
were not glued together but rather were screwed
together at strategic points with machine screws. Since
the model was constantly being assembled and disassembled as various aspects of the work were completed, a consistent method of fastening and alignment
had to be developed. Wherever the opportunity presented itself for a screw to be fastened to the top of a

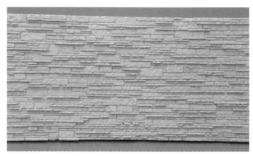

ABOVE: **View of stone wall used to create the master model for the rubber mold with 12-inch ruler in place.** LEFT: **Rubber mold of stone wall.** RIGHT: **Casting of a stonewall.**

core wall or above one of the fireplaces, the model would be connected at that point. Screws would be found underneath furniture, in closets, within fireplaces or under the stone coping of walls. Screwing the model together rather than gluing allowed it to expand and contract with temperature changes and to be painted prior to assembly.

CASTING STONE WALLS

One of the many unknowns encountered during the analysis of how the model would be constructed was the stone bearing walls. Obviously it would have been

impossible to build the model with miniature stones assembled and glued together against the core wall. Duplicating the stone pattern and producing the number of individual stones necessary would be impractical and time consuming. Therefore, a representative large section of wall surface was chosen at Fallingwater, which was photographed with a twelve-inch ruler resting vertically on a stone ledge. This photograph was then enlarged until the ruler in the photograph was 3/8 inch long. Now, the photo represented a section of stone wall at the proper scale of 3/8 inch equaling one foot. A thin piece of plastic was laid over this photo and individual pieces of plastic, in various thicknesses, were glued to this surface. The projection of the various stones relative to each other was duplicated in scale. The sample used was 4 inches by 10 inches. When each stone in the photo was covered by a piece of plastic, the surface of that plastic stone was carved and rendered to duplicate the texture of each stone surface. Rendering was accomplished through use of a Dremel tool and a series of various-sized ball cutters used to create the subtleties of the stone surface. When this master model was completed, a rubber mold was made which accurately reproduced in negative relief each nuance of the stones. The mold was placed in a support tray and was then ready for casting.

MoMA's Fallingwater model has walls made of a mix of 50% plaster of Paris and 50% dental plaster. This ratio was arrived at after trial and error to achieve the right amount of hardness and workability of the surface. Once the formula for this mix of plaster and the proper amount of water was developed, it was then a matter of casting as many sheets of stone walls as necessary for the model. It should be noted that a vibrating machine was used after pouring the plaster into the mold to insure that there would be no air bubbles and that every crevice of the mold was filled.

The 1987 Monaghan model used a different material for the stone walls. Those walls utilized a type of casting plastic called Repro 83, that consisted of a Part "A" and Part "B" mixture, which chemically bonded to each other. This blue-colored material could be machined like acrylic, since it possessed many of the same capabilities as sheet acrylic.

LEFT: **Sample of a typical corner of a stone wall using a butt-joint.**
BELOW: **Third Floor bedroom fireplace.**

DEVELOPING A STONE
RENDERING METHODOLOGY

Fallingwater has stone floors as well as stone walls. When the house was photographed during the initial documentation phase, many of the rooms were photographed showing the pattern of stonework on the floor. It was easier to replicate the actual stone pattern than to design ones own pattern. When the entire Fallingwater model was completed in its "clear" form, that is, entirely in acrylic with smooth floors and only core walls supporting the floors, each floor was rendered like stone. In order to render the stone floors, a light hand sanding of the acrylic surface was applied, scuffing it enough so that one could draw the pattern of the stone floor on the surface. After this pattern was drawn, comparing it to the photographs and other source material with different views, a special tool was used to carve the groove of the joints. The actual joints in Fallingwater are recessed from the stone surface. The Dremel tool did not work well in carving these joints. However, a table-top version of a dentist's drill, powered by an electric motor driving cables over pulleys and controlled with a foot pedal, provided the right amount of speed and sensitivity. Using a variety of 1/16-inch diameter and smaller ball cutters and arrowhead shaped cutters, it was possible to cut grooves in varying widths simulating the mortar joints between the stones. When this tedious process was completed

the outline of the stone pattern was very evident but the surface of each stone was still perfectly flat.

Now, with the use of a Dremel tool and larger ball cutters, it was possible to carve the distinctive texture of each stone into the surface of the acrylic. As the texture approached the joint, an uneven joint edge was created exactly as the stonework in the actual house. After much study of photos of the stone floors, I noticed that there were about three or four basic patterns of texture in the stone. I soon learned to imitate this texture during my carving process, in some cases

BELOW: **View of the three-step process towards rendering the floors, pencil outline of the stones, cutting the groove of the joints, rendering the surface.**

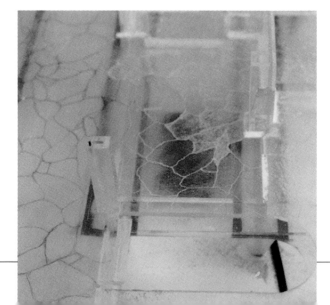

TOP: **The living room hearth boulder.** BOTTOM: **Living room stone floor pattern, displaying various types of texture.**

skipping the cutter lightly over sharp edges and creating a whole level of patterns very similar to the actual stones. Again, this was a very time consuming, tedious, monotonous process, but the results were spectacular. The bearing walls, which are made of stone, utilized a completely different technique. Recall that the walls of the model were core walls to which a pre-cast plaster laminate of cast stone pattern would be glued. This 4-inch by 10-inch wall was made in two thicknesses, one at 1/4-inch thick and another at 1/8-inch thick. This single 4-inch by 10-inch wall pattern is used throughout the Fallingwater model. At times it would be upside down, but every effort was made to alter the pattern so that it was never obvious that one pattern existed. The plaster stone-patterned sheet was cut with a special composite circular blade in the table saw with a simple series of PVC pipes connected to a vacuum cleaner to collect the dust as the material was cut. The stone sheet was fitted and cut to fit against one side of the core wall. Either Krazy Glue or a special mix of solvent and plastic particles forming a paste were used to attach the plaster to the acrylic.

The corners of the stone walls presented other problems. I rejected a mitered joint in favor of a butt joint, which not only provided a stronger gluing surface but also enabled me to re-carve the cut end of the wall to blend in with the stone adjacent to it. The horizontal joint was reestablished with a small jigsaw blade. A white putty used for marine applications made by Interlux was used to fill in stone joints when they did not align perfectly around the corner. This putty was also used to fill in joints in order to recarve several stones into one larger stone. Fallingwater, the house, when carefully studied, will reveal a slightly different stone pattern from the lower level to the higher level. Apparently, different groups of stone masons worked on each level of the house, with larger patterned stones used at the lowest levels. Also, Wright was fond of using much larger stones at corners or at the base of walls to give a sense of carrying the weight of the floors above. Where possible, these larger stones were done in the model, particularly if I had a photo showing a larger stone on the wall I was working on at the time. This singular process of gluing the stone sheets to the core walls, recarving the corners of each wall, and altering the pattern of the stonework was six months long.

THE HANGING STAIRCASE

Fallingwater has two rather elegant hanging staircases, which are composed of three-inch-thick concrete steps suspended from the ceiling by metal straps. One stairway leads from the first floor living room level to the third floor. The other is the more recognizable staircase from the living room down to a platform suspended inches above the Bear Run stream. This is the

Hanging steps to the stream.

staircase suspended by a series of metal straps from the primary horizontal cantilevered floor above the waterfall. Constructing these staircases was a very delicate matter involving a rather complicated jig, which held the steps in position while the straps were inserted. Once the stairs were fully assembled, they were then lifted, while in the jig, into a series of corresponding holes, where they were bent into a channel and anchored. Thus, when the jig was disassembled, the stairs truly hung there. The chapter on jigs will elaborate this process in more detail.

3

SITE CONSTRUCTION
THE LAY OF THE LAND

THE BASE SUPERSTRUCTURE

The model of Fallingwater would not be complete without the land from which it grows. This is what Frank Lloyd Wright meant when he spoke about organic architecture. The model, therefore, had to be anchored to a base, and that base would support the landscape, trees, waterfall, and streambed. It was decided that this base would be no larger than four feet by six feet, since that size adequately showed the topographical changes of the Fallingwater site and was of sufficient size for display purposes in the museum's galleries.

The base of the Fallingwater model was built from various levels of 3/4-inch-thick plywood. Careful measurements were made from a survey drawing showing the positioning of the house in the landscape, relative to the stream and the waterfall. Beginning with the base of the waterfall, a platform was built of plywood, with supporting sides and cross members. Next, the upper stream level of the waterfall was built on a platform about 8 inches above the last one. A smaller level above the Bear Run stream matched the elevation of the bridge leading to the roadway behind the house. And finally a level beyond and above the roadway completed the structure. The plywood base now

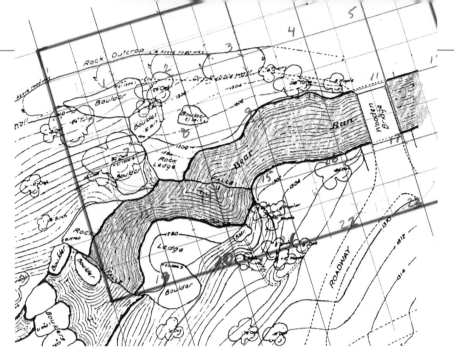

appeared as a series of steps with hollow areas within serving as access ways to screws fastening the very foundations of the model.

This space-frame type structure is very rigid, will not warp and provides a very solid base for supporting the model. Finally, the sides of the base were also covered in plywood, making the entire structure ready for the landscape.

FOAM LAMINATIONS

With the plywood base levels completed, styrofoam layers were glued into place in thicknesses corresponding to the contour map. There are various ways to construct sloping topography. Methods such as plaster cloths or papier-mache are simply not controllable enough to reproduce such a recognizable landscape as Fallingwater. The use of foam boards, such as urethane or styrofoam, enables one to carve the forms precisely. In other models, I often used urethane foam, which

is very porous and easy to carve. It does break down into fine dust, and one must wear a mask. Also, the particles tend to cling to clothing due to static electricity. It was decided to use styrofoam, the more rigid kind used as insulation on foundation walls. This type of foam can be machined and easily sanded. Any gouges can be filled with joint compound, the ready-mixed plaster used to seal sheetrock joints. When the final form of the landscape was completed, a layer of joint compound sealed the foam and provided a very good base for painting. The Fallingwater model was carved with a combination of a router, which followed the contours of the survey drawing, and hand sanding, which eliminated the stepping of this technique and produced a more natural look.

ROCK FORMATIONS

Fallingwater is such a world famous house, and so recognizable, that even the rock formations are famous. The sandstone ledge over which the waterfall flows and the other rock formations beneath it have their own identities. They had to be shaped with the same care and attention to detail as the house. All the major boulders and ledges surrounding Fallingwater were pho-

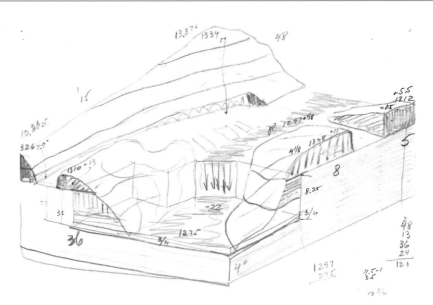

tographed from various angles. Some were measured, particularly those which merged with the house and became a part of the architecture. The top of the boulder in the living room, which is both the hearth of the fireplace and the rock around which Fallingwater was built, was carefully measured and replicated exactly. The top of this boulder was made of acrylic and glued onto the floor. However, all other boulders against the house or surrounding the house, including the ledges beneath the waterfall, were made of rigid styrofoam covered and further detailed with joint compound. The joint compound adheres very well to the blue or pink styrofoam, providing detail and a good base for painting. The other rock formation that was critical to the model was the external expression of the living room boulder, which connected with the kitchen and formed a ledge at the base of the tall vertical window. Another important and prominent boulder was at the bottom of the western-most terrace of the house. This boulder has three transverse beams, which anchor into the rock and serve to assist in the cantilever of this terrace.

This rock was carved out of solid foam and fitted into the beams of the model. It was also detailed with the characteristic striations and texture that the boulder possesses.

HOW THE HOUSE MEETS THE SITE

At some point, the model of the house, which was independently constructed with each floor stacked upon the other and all resting on the cellar or foundation level, has to meet the site. The base, which had been independently constructed according to the survey, had to receive the very foundation of the model in order to fully merge it with the site. This part of the foundation is both one edge of the stream at Bear Run and the retaining wall for the roadway on the north side of the house. This is also the level where the house merges with the three large boulders upon which it is built. The foundation level is particularly noticeable as the wall containing the plunge pool, which defines the stream and frames the hanging staircase. The plunge pool has a spout of water projecting from its eastern wall that creates a ripple effect, which mimics the stream. The model had now reached the point where the house was inseparable from the base.

4

WATER RENDERING TECHNIQUES

HOW "DO" YOU BUILD A WATERFALL

THE STREAM AT BEAR RUN

As was suggested in the very beginning of this book, one of the unknowns that I faced in constructing this model was the convincing rendering of the stream. Water is a moving phenomenon, a reality unsuited for an architectural model representing a moment in time. Achieving the dynamism of moving water captured, as one would in a photograph, without making it look like frozen water would prove to be a challenge. Research in various model railroad magazines proved futile. It was difficult to find any articles that involved the use of water in model railroad layouts, let alone any descriptions of techniques to render water. However, eventually I did find an article in a model railroad publication that, to my surprise, described rendering a river and a waterfall. The author recommended using resin, which could be

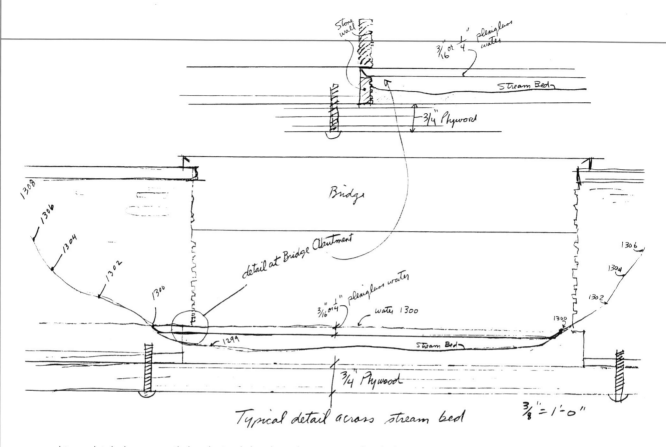

Stone wall

$3/16$" or $1/4$" plexiglass water

Stream Bed

$3/4$" Plywood

Bridge

detail at Bridge Abutment

1308

1306

1304

1302

1300

1299

$3/16$" or $1/4$" plexiglass water

water 1300

Stream Bed

1306

1304

1302

1300

$3/4$" Plywood

Typical detail across stream bed $3/8$" = 1'-0"

poured in multiple layers until the desired depth and effect were achieved. The problem with resin is several fold. For one, it requires the addition of a catalyst, which is added in drops, thoroughly mixed into the medium, and eventually hardens the resin. The addition of the hardener is imprecise and results in a varying hardness of the final product. Also, resin shrinks as it cures and over time can actually craze or crack as the various layers cure at different rates. Pouring the resin would require an absolutely level model base, which is not difficult to do, and some kind of edging to contain it.

Pouring the stream would also presuppose that the painting of the streambed had been completed. Any error in pouring the resin could ruin months of work.

Indeed, the most convincing feature of the rendering of the Bear Run stream would be achieving the effect of flowing water by reproducing the ripples and wavelets of moving water. This effect is impossible with a material such as resin, which sets up in a short amount of time and in a pour that is three feet long and as much as a half inch thick. The rhythmic subtlety of the ripples and waves is impossible in this medium. Even if the effect was successful, within a year's time the edges of the stream would shrink and leave a gap between the shoreline and the water. It was therefore necessary to begin with a stable material in order to replicate the water.

The obvious, and my reluctant choice, was acrylic sheet. It is clear and has limited movement, due to tem-

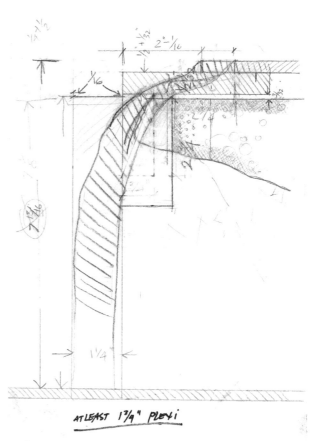

AT LEAST 1³/₄" PLEXI

OPPOSITE PAGE: **Scale drawing of the section of the stream at the bridge abutments.**
ABOVE: **Section drawing for the waterfall and sample for lucite waterfall carving.**

perature rather than chemical reaction. Any shrinkage would have already occurred at the factory. The acrylic comes in different thicknesses and can be carved and polished. In fact, after several test pieces, carving and polishing proved to be best technique for the stream. Another difficult aspect was reproducing the patterns of the stream, with its systems and subsystems of waves and ripples. The stream actually had to be de-signed and the pattern superimposed on the acrylic. A pattern for the design of the stream was placed beneath a precut sheet of acrylic representing the stream. With this drawing beneath the sheet, the pattern could be carved above it.

The carving was done with a Dremel tool and a 1/4-inch-diameter ball cutter, to carve tiny ripples as valleys and peaks in the acrylic sheet. This technique is similar to the stone-carving portions, except that the design is different and flowing. After countless hours of this tedious process, the carved stream was no longer transparent and had to be polished to restore its luster and transparency. It was a forgiving procedure, since any perceived mistakes could be carved over and repolished.

Polishing was achieved with a buffing wheel and a special rouge used for acrylic. The polishing was also a tedious process, using a buffing wheel that was only 1/2-inch thick, to reach into the valleys of the ripples. This could not be done by hand and required a good buffing machine to achieve the results. An interesting product of the method was the smoothing and rounding of the sharp edge between the valleys by the buffing wheel, further enhancing the effect of water.

THAT FAMOUS WATERFALL

The waterfall construction proved to be a real challenge and another of the unknowns of the model. The technique for rendering the waterfall was similar to the one developed for the stream. Once again, it became a question of taking a pattern and imposing that pattern into the acrylic. While the pattern of the stream was one of a flowing mass moving horizontally, the waterfall would be a flowing mass falling vertically. Studying photos of the waterfall, particularly as the streams of water flowed over the sandstone ledge, revealed a particular form. Just as the landscape had a character, so did the waterfall.

In order to capture the thrust of the waterfall as it flowed over and beyond the ledge, a rather thick piece of acrylic had to be used. Also, the waterfall, when viewed from above was concave, reflecting the curve of the ledge. Therefore, three 1 1/4-inch-thick pieces of acrylic, at the proper height, were segmented together. The carving took place from the back portion of the top and ended at the front portion at the bottom. Carving took place on the front surface, as well as the rear surface. A small flat surface at the top allowed gluing to the edge of the stream so that the flow

would appear as one surface of water flowing across and over the falls. The waterfall was not glued at the bottom where it attaches to the lower portion of the stream. The reason for allowing the waterfall to "float" at this point was to permit any expansion or contraction along the length of the upper stream.

The entire effect of the carving and the polishing of the waterfall was to capture flowing water, not frozen water. Absolute clarity and minimizing of the thickness helped, but the setting of the waterfall in its surroundings convinced the mind to believe that this is a moment in time of a body of flowing water. The most difficult and perhaps unsuccessful part of the illusion was the base of the falls. It is impossible to render the mist of bouncing water as it strikes the rocks below. A vertical, rendered piece of acrylic meets a horizontal, rendered piece of acrylic; blurring this joint is difficult. Recently, a product called aerogel, which is the lightest solid ever developed, came to mind as a solution for this situation. Although it is extremely expensive and hard to obtain, I thought that shaping this transparent yet solid material might be the way to suggest the misting that occurs at the base of a waterfall.

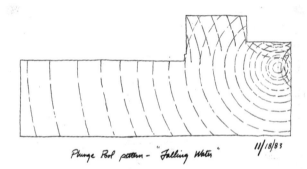

TOP LEFT: **3/8-inch scale drawing and study for the plunge pool water patterns. When the patterns were determined, this drawing was placed under a sheet of acrylic and guided the carving of the ripples.** TOP RIGHT: **The finished 1/16-inch thick acrylic plunge pool pattern after carving and polishing.** ABOVE: **View of the plunge pool inserted in place along recessed slots in the stone walls. The model's plunge pool was positioned from the stream side and locked into place when the stone coping of the perimeter wall was glued.**

PLUNGE POOLS

The plunge pool is located at the very lowest elevation of Fallingwater, alongside the stream. The plunge pool is framed by a low stone wall between the base platform of the hanging staircase and a retaining wall supporting the roadway. The plunge pool is accessed from a stair off the main entrance. The pool is about four feet deep and its bottom is at a similar elevation as the bottom of the stream. A singular feature of the plunge pool is a spout of water emerging from its east wall and into the pool. A smaller pool with a similar spout is north of the entrance door. The effect of the spout is to form an expanding series of concentric circles of ripples emanating from the point of contact with the water. In terms of the model, this was a wholly different pattern of waves to be carved. It was neither flowing water nor falling water, but rather "still" water with a singular source of undulations.

In order to replicate the pattern of ripples, partic-ularly since the pool is a long, irregular rectangle, it was necessary to make a small model. I took a shallow aluminum tray and outlined the shape of the pool with metal blocks. I filled the tray with water and gently tapped one end of the water's surface with a pencil at the point where the spout entered the water. I was then able to study the pattern of waves as they eman-ated from this point, hit various walls, and bounced back. I observed the spacing, as well as the counter pattern caused by the wall outline.

Once the pattern was fully understood, it was drawn on a piece of paper at the same scale and size as the model. This pattern was then placed under a 1/16-inch-thick piece of acrylic sheet and carved and polished with the same technique used for the stream and waterfall. The spout became a thin nylon monofilament (the kind used with fishing rod reels), which was placed into a small hole in the stone wall. The spout terminated in a similar hole in the carved acrylic sheet. The curve of the thrust of the water spout was created by controlling the length of the nylon monofilament.

5

FURNITURE CONSTRUCTION

AS ONLY WRIGHT COULD DESIGN IT

BUILT-IN ELEMENTS

Fallingwater has its own distinctive furniture design, whose lines are often inspired by the broad cantilevered massing of the house itself. All of the bedrooms, the dining room and the living room have built-in furniture elements that are intrinsic to the space.

These elements not only define the space but control movement through it. As in the actual house, the model's furniture had to be built into the space. Many pieces were cut to fit into stone or to wrap around stone columns. However, drawings of the furniture were not supplied, and measurements had to be taken

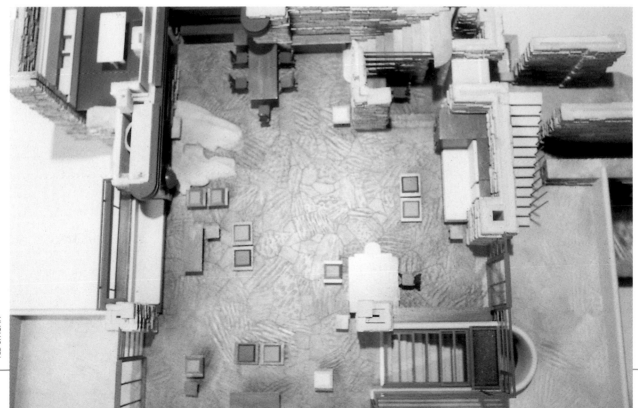

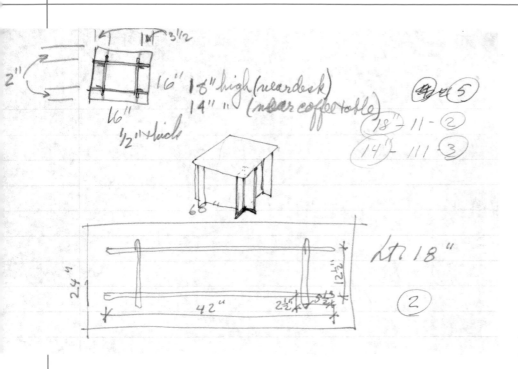

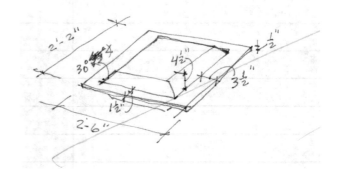

from the actual pieces. The model's furniture was made of mostly 1/32-inch-thick acrylic, fitted into finished but unpainted rooms, and then later painted.

INDIVIDUAL PIECES

There are several ottomans and small tables that comprise the living room furniture. These pieces were built from actual measurements of the furniture and built in a similar fashion to the built-in elements. The dining room chairs, which were not designed by Wright but chosen by the Kaufmanns, were also built, because they have always been a part of Fallingwater from the very beginning. The kitchen cabinets, sink, and stove were also built as well as the kitchen table, which was designed by Wright. All of these individual pieces were built in like fashion.

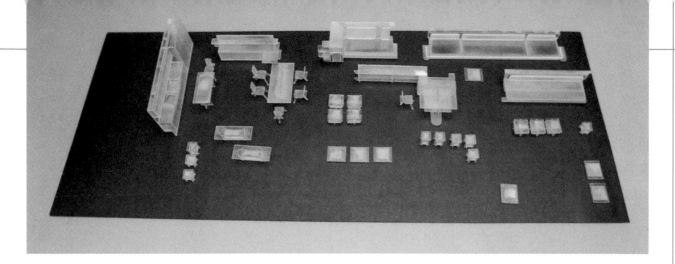

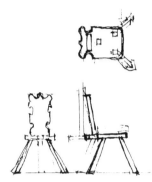

ABOVE: **Clear acrylic array of furniture for the first floor of the model.** BELOW: **Dining room chairs, the only non-Wright designed furniture in Fallingwater.**

6

WINDOW & EXTERIOR DOOR CONSTRUCTION

A CHALLENGE

WINDOWS AND DOORS IN STONE OPENINGS

Fallingwater has casement windows made of thin square metal tubing. The framing is so narrow and of such long horizontal dimensions that it appears that the glass itself helps to support these wide expanses. Fallingwater uses very thin glass framed by layers of metal tubing, which in section expresses the mullion, and a recessed frame, which holds the glass in place. To achieve this effect in the model, it was necessary to begin with thin 1/32-inch-thick acrylic as the window and glue onto the surface a thin strip of styrene representing the total width of the window frames. Along the centerline of this piece was glued a thinner-layer of styrene, representing the furthest projection of the frame. This technique was utilized on both sides of the acrylic window so that the effect was a thin piece of glass supported by a narrow-section square tube of metal. Additional laminations were used where casement win-

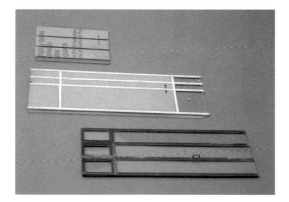

dows occurred. Even a horizontal ledge of metal at the base of each casement window was expressed by a thin piece of lexan sheet. Once painted, the overall effect captured the texture and relief of the window framing.

The windows and doors in Fallingwater are also built into the stonework. This presented an interesting challenge in the model: to produce the effect of a built-in window or doorframe. There is also a Wright detail, which has a sheet of glass going directly into the stone without benefit of any framing.

The task was even more difficult since the stonework phase of the model had to be performed on each floor as it was completed, that is, each floor's stonework was built only after the prior floor was completed. This was a six-month process. The windows

TOP: Window samples in various stages of construction.
BOTTOM: Window detail directly into a stone wall without benefit of framing.

were to be built afterwards. Taking a lesson from actual construction in stone, window frames, window slots, and doorframes were provided for as the stonework was glued into position. In other words, a groove of the correct width was machined into the stonework with a milling tool on a drill press, and then a frame in acrylic was precut and fitted into it and left there until painting.

This process allowed the stonework to continue uninterrupted. Where applicable, the entire window or door and frame could be slid into the top of the wall of each floor, locked in place by the succeeding floor above. The tall three-story vertical window embracing the kitchen and bedrooms above was built as one piece and slid into position after assembly of the model, and locked in position by the roof. This window is fitted into a continuous vertical groove alongside the exterior of the chimney without benefit of any framing, exactly as Wright detailed it.

WINDOWS IN CONCRETE RAILINGS

Fallingwater is a stone and concrete structure. Inevitably, as the internal spaces progress from stone enclosures to concrete and glass enclosures, window-framing progresses from stone to concrete. The spaces facing the south are enclosed by concrete railings and glass. In Fallingwater, the metal framing of the windows sits exactly on the centerline of the curved top of the concrete railing. In the model, this concrete railing was slight-

ly less than 3/16-inch thick. Gluing a thin window onto this surface was extremely difficult. The solution was to cut a thin groove into the top of the railing, approximately 1/8-inch deep, and wide enough to accept a 1/32-inch-thick sheet of acrylic representing the window. This slotted rail then accepted along its length, the bottom portion of the window, covered by the window framing on either side. The technique, executed by a thin saw blade cutting at a measured depth, produced an effect that mimicked the original.

7

JIGS

HELPING HANDS

THE LIVING ROOM CURVED STAIR RAIL

A "jig" is a plate or a device, such as an open frame or box, which holds a work in position while certain operations are performed on it. Jigs are often used to perform repetitive operations. But jigs may also be used to build only one piece of work. Jigs can be very simple forms around which a piece is bent or they can be more com-

plicated, composed of several interlocking components.

Any bent or curved element made of acrylic must be heated and held in a form until it cools. Once cooled, it will retain the curvature of the form. In Fallingwater, a curved concrete stair rail serves as the opening for the hanging staircase leading to the stream below. As noted before, the concrete railing elements in the Fallingwater

model were made of acrylic of 3/16-inch thickness and curved on the top edge. In order to bend the living-room railing, it was necessary to heat the portion of the railing that was to be curved. Commercial strip heaters are available, which consist of a heated wire over which the portion to be bent is laid. However, the curvature of this railing was large. The simplest way to bend it was to cover in aluminum foil those portions of the railing to remain straight. The curved portion was left exposed. By placing the piece in a small toaster

oven, it was possible to soften the acrylic. At the appropriate softness, the piece was removed and wrapped around a wooden form and held by flat metal plates until cooled. Submerging it in cold water hastened the cooling process.

Once completed, the railing was trimmed and fit into place. Any distortions in the curved portion of the railing were corrected by sanding and filling with automobile glazing and spot putty. This was a relatively simple jig.

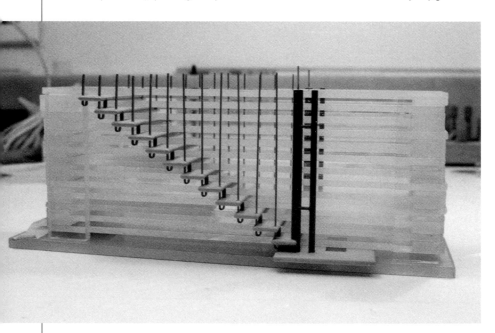

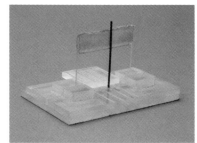

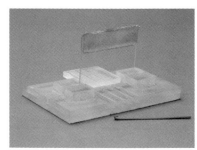

THE HANGING STAIRCASE TO BEAR RUN

A more complicated jig involved the construction of the hanging staircase. The hanging staircase is a suspended series of steps from the living room to the stream. The steps are a series of individually suspended stair treads, culminating in a suspended platform hovering about 12 inches above the surface of the stream. The steps are concrete and suspended by a series of flat metal straps, each of which engages the front portion of one step and the rear portion of the step below. Each step is supported by two straps on each end. The straps are all embedded in the concrete slab above. The straps penetrate each step and terminate in a U shape below the step. The platform, while appearing to be suspended, is in fact supported by a series of vertical metal angles anchored both in the top slab and into the streambed. The platform is then cantilevered from this support. The steps are 2-inch-thick reinforced concrete slabs while the platform is a 3-inch-thick reinforced concrete slab.

Nevertheless, constructing a jig to build this staircase was quite a challenge. Several jigs were built for various sections of the staircase. Then, a separate jig had to be constructed to hold all the elements in place while the staircase was assembled.

The first operation entailed cutting a long thin strip of acrylic at the depth of the steps. A special cutter, attached to a router table, transformed the flat edge into a curved semi-circular surface.

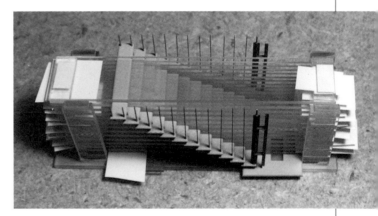

This continuous strip was then cut to the correct width of each step. Then, the ends of each step received the same semi-circular surface treatment.

A separate jig held each step in position so that a thin slot could be cut with a small circular blade. Two slots at either end of each step would allow a thin brass strap to be inserted to the correct depth. Another series of slots provided a separate, smaller vertical strap further supporting one step to the other.

The ends of each strap terminated in a U shaped configuration. A separate jig was built which would

RIGHT: **The other hanging staircase from the first floor to the second floor.** BELOW: **The hanging staircase now permanently in place and prior to removal of the jig.** BELOW CENTER: **View of the top of the straps prior to bending in the slot.**

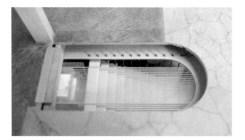

place this bend simultaneously in four straps at the same time. The jig allowed four thin brass straps to be laid horizontally within a supporting groove. At the end of this groove was a gap and a stop. A guillotine type of operation would allow a thin piece of plastic to be pressed into this gap and force the U shape into the ends of the four brass strips.

Another jig supported the array of angles and flat straps that comprise the support columns for the platform. This jig held everything in position so that the individual joints could be soldered.

At the point of attachment of the top of the straps into the slab above, it was necessary to drill a series of holes to allow passage of the straps through

the acrylic. A flat piece of acrylic with a series of holes aligned with the tops of each strap was built to serve as the pattern for drilling these holes into the supporting slab.

With the completion of all of the components, comprising the hanging steps, it was then necessary to devise a jig that would support all these pieces while they were glued to each other. The solution was a series of flat pieces of acrylic, representing the space between the steps, which were supported at either end and held in alignment by two vertical supports at each end. By inserting the individual steps between these supporting pieces it was then possible to take an individual brass strap and insert it into the slots at the end of each step. Each strap was cut to the proper length allowing for penetration into the holes of the supporting slab above. As each strap was placed in the aligned slots of each step, the series of steps became a rigid structure. When the plumbness of each strap was established, a dab of Krazy Glue in the stair slot fixed the position. When all steps were completed, the remainder of the slot was filled with marine putty, which further secured the strap and was sanded to conform to the end of the step. The platform's sup-

porting columns were also fixed in a like manner and completed the entire assembly. The entire assembled hanging staircase was then within the clutches of the jig. By carefully sliding out each horizontal element of the jig, in alternate fashion the entire staircase was released from the jig and remained alone as a completed yet delicate assemblage.

At the appropriate time in the model's process of completion, this hanging staircase assemblage was painted. It was then replaced inside the jig assembly and

FAR LEFT: **Central stairway railing and planter.**
NEAR LEFT: **The two hanging staircases in painted and completed form.**
BELOW: **Rear view of the plastic jig for the second floor railing.**

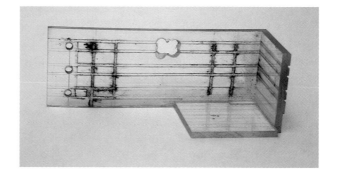

lifted into position so that the ends of each strap would penetrate its corresponding hole in the slab above.

Once all the straps were in place, they were individually bent into a pre-cut groove inside the floor. When the curved rail was dropped into position above the staircase, it locked the straps in the groove. The staircase then hung by itself just as in the original house.

THE HANGING STEPS TO THE SECOND FLOOR

A similar series of hanging steps connects the main level of the house to the second floor. This series of steps is constructed in a similar fashion to the hanging steps from the living room to the stream. The steps are only about 30 inches wide, with the exposed side hung by metal straps from the ceiling slab above and the other end of the steps supported by the stone wall.

In terms of the model, these steps were built with the same jig used to construct the hanging staircase. However, since one end of these steps is supported by the stone wall, another jig was required for cutting a series of slotted openings matching the section of each step so that it could be inserted into the stone wall of the model.

TOP: **The hanging staircase.** BOTTOM: **Detail view of supporting metal straps for the hanging staircase, and metal column support for the platform.** OPPOSITE PAGE TOP: **Brass models of railings, living room kettle and fireplace grating.** OPPOSITE PAGE BOTTOM: **View of fireplace grating.**

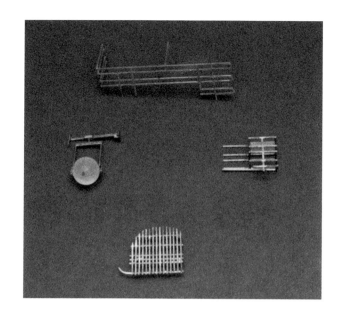

METAL RAILINGS

There are only two metal railings in Fallingwater. One is at the inside central stairway, which also supports a planter, and the other is outside at the level of the second floor, enclosing the opening of the smaller set of hanging steps. A jig was constructed for each one of these railings. In addition, jigs were constructed for the living room fireplace grating and the supports for the cauldron positioned within the fireplace.

The approach in constructing these jigs was to use acrylic forms cut with grooves to accept the brass pieces used for either the railings or grating, thereby holding them in position for soldering. While the plastic will burn at these joints, it is of no consequence since the jigs are not used more than once. Constructing them in wood was unnecessary, although it is the preferred medium. Acrylic is expedient, since it glues together quickly. After the piece has been soldered, the provision of holes at non-joint locations facilitates popping the finished product out of the jig. Then the process of filing and sanding begins, in order to remove excess solder from the joints. At this point, the finished piece is fitted into position and awaits painting and final assembly.

8

PAINTING THE BUILDING
THE PALETTE IS NOT JUST CHEROKEE RED

CONCRETE COLORS

The palette of colors used in Fallingwater was generally earth tones, which reflected the colors of the landscape surrounding the house. The streambed, ground cover, native stone, and colors of the tree limbs all contributed to the colors used in Fallingwater. All of the concrete portions of the building represented by the railings, trellises, hanging steps, and the edges of flat roofs were painted in a beige color. The Western Pennsylvania Conservancy, which is in charge of the property of Fallingwater and conducts tours there, supplied color samples for the concrete. The beige color was a mix of various quantities of flat lacquer, which was sprayed over a gray lacquer primer. The color consisted primarily of white flat lacquer with measured quantities of raw sien-

View of the north elevation of the model at the level of the roadway with the cellar retaining wall visible and the first and second floors.

na, gray, and bright red. Mixing color is an art form and requires the ability to see various colors within a particular color. By estimating and testing various quantities of these colors, one can arrive in the neighborhood of the color to be matched. It is easier to stay on the lighter side because if it becomes too dark it is difficult to return to a lighter shade. Once the closest approximation of the color is attained it must be fully dried in order to compare the match. Lacquer colors often dry darker than when they are in the wet stage. If a sample is provided, a dab of paint on the sample should disappear once it has dried; this indicates a perfect match.

STONE FLOORS

The walking surfaces of Fallingwater, that is, the interior floor surfaces and the exterior terraces, are paved in stone. The same stone quarried for the supporting walls was also cut for stone pavers. Wright distin-

TED SPAGNA

RIGHT: **Interior view of the living room fireplace and hearth. Wall detail at the level of the west terrace.** OPPOSITE PAGE: **Sample of the wood graining technique on acrylic.**

TED SPAGNA

guished the interior spaces from the exterior spaces by providing a sealer and wax for all interior walking surfaces. The sealer gave a wet appearance and a finishing touch that was not extended to individual stone stair treads. The living room boulder was also spared this finish and appears to emerge as a peninsula surrounded by a vast sea.

Painting the floors and terraces of the model of Fallingwater required a palette of colors including white, raw umber, burnt umber, black, gray, and yellow-brown. The floors were first painted in a light gray lacquer primer. The type of paint used was a water-based tempera or gouache, which proved to be very suitable over the gray primer. Since the floor was carved in a highly textured stone finish, it was very easy to apply a general light brown tone to the floors and then highlight areas with shades of gray and tones of brown. By applying the tempera with a brush and daubing it with a cloth, a very natural looking effect of stone color was achieved. As each stone was painted in a slightly different shade than the other, it was possible to cover large areas rather quickly. To achieve the effect of the finished interior floor, a semi-gloss wash of a clear paint was used together with slightly darker colors than were used in the exterior terraces. The effect matched the actual floor and terrace finishes. The painting technique required a very uninhibited approach, controlled but not careless.

STONE WALLS

The stone walls of the model had the same paint and painting technique as the floors. As with the floors, individual stones were painted by daubing them only after a general wash of a gray-brown color was applied to the entire surface. By going back to individual stones with varying shades of brown, white, and gray, a visual texture of color was achieved. The technique gave a certain vitality to the wall that was very natural looking. The tempera used was also highly diluted in water. It is important to understand that the paint was not absorbed by the stone material, but rather applied over the primer, which had already sealed the surface.

FURNITURE WOODGRAINING SECRETS

The furniture at Fallingwater is walnut-veneered plywood. Many of the veneers are streaked with sapwood, which normally would be rejected. But Wright liked these streaks and chose to run them horizontally to continue the horizontal theme of the house. The model was fully detailed with all the built-in furniture and includes beds, desks, and ottomans. Even the doors to bedrooms, which are also of walnut, were included.

Developing a rendering technique to simulate this wood graining proved to be a real challenge. The furniture was built of clear acrylic. It was then primed with gray lacquer and ready for a wood painting technique. Various methods were tried that proved unsuccessful. To achieve the wood graining, one method used a basic color of gold paint, with a variety of brown paint applied over it with visible brush strokes. This method was unconvincing, even though it is similar to actual techniques used in faux graining on real doors. The technique did not provide the depth that real graining has or the lustre of natural wood. A certain vitality was missing.

In searching for appropriate walnut-colored paints I came across metallic paints used for touching up finishes on automobiles. A dark cordovan metallic acrylic lacquer closely resembled the color, but was too red. A golden brown metallic acrylic lacquer was too yellow. However, when these two colors were sprayed together the color appeared just right, except that there was no graining.

Since the grain was of a yellow or golden hue, I tried streaking over this combined color with gold enamel paint. The effect was unsuccessful and the streaking was obviously applied over the wood color and was not an intrinsic part of the paint. I then realized that the technique lied in first spraying one color, then streaking the gold graining, and then applying the second color. This process achieved two results. Spraying any lacquer over enamel had the effect of melting the enamel. Therefore applying the second color over the first with the gold streaks simultaneously melted or softened the gold streaking and mixed with the first color to produce the walnut color. The effect was to have a subtle graining effect with the deep lustre of what in model form looked like walnut veneer. The slightly metallic quality of the paint also imparted a texture and depth to the furniture that was very effective. The technique was simple and very fast. But spray cans were not used, only the airbrush, and any mistakes could be easily corrected by simply streaking more gold paint and applying more or less of each of the two colors involved.

WINDOW FRAMES AND CHEROKEE RED

The Western Pennsylvania Conservancy supplied me with a quart of Cherokee Red paint used at Fallingwater. A mixture of lacquers was produced which matched the color of the enamel paint supplied. Cherokee Red, which resembles a terracotta color, is a mixture of burnt sienna and red. In lacquer form, this color was applied by airbrush to the built up laminations of styrene, which had already been primed in light gray. A lacquer version of this color rather than the actual enamel version was easier to spray onto the fine detailing of the window moldings, dries quickly and leaves a very smooth finish.

9

PAINTING
THE LANDSCAPE

IMITATING MOTHER NATURE

STREAMBEDS

With the complete lamination of the base with styrofoam and an applied coating of joint compound, the streambed was ready for painting. The stream in the immediate vicinity of the hanging stairs and just before the waterfall is quite shallow. The streambed is also very muddy although the water is clear. A light brown layer of gouache was applied to the streambed. Various darker and lighter shades of a gray-brown color were applied to give texture to the bed as well as to reflect through the textured water above. The color modulations gave a certain depth and liveliness to the stream once it was completed. Any rocks or debris that were under the water were then carefully positioned.

The stream was a rendered and polished piece of 1/4-inch-thick acrylic sheet fitted into position along

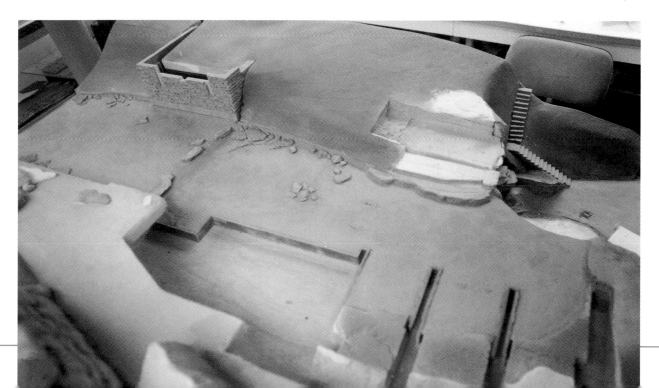

ABOVE: The stream is now sealed above the stream bed and the shoreline is plastered in and eventually painted. LEFT: The sandstone ledges and boulders near the base of the waterfall. OPPOSITE PAGE: The boulder supporting the western-most terrace with embedded concrete beams.

the edges of the streambed. The bottom edge of the acrylic stream was curved and polished so that the interface of the stream's edge with the shoreline would be as thin as possible. Once the acrylic stream was in place, forever sealing the streambed, the shoreline was plastered up to the edge of the water. This edge was sanded and painted to match the surrounding surface.

ROCK PAINTING

The boulders and the sandstone ledges that create the waterfall, as well as the various smaller rocks that are at the base of the falls, were all painted in a similar fashion as the stone walls of the house. A tempera paint was applied over plaster, which sealed the styrofoam rocks. The painted boulders near the waterfall received a clear coating, which replicated the constant state of wetness on their surfaces. Other rocks throughout the site and along the road behind the house were also built of styrofoam and given a texture with the plaster coating. Every effort was made to duplicate the shape and relative sizes of each boulder to one another. Even the texture and surface detail of the larger boulders were rendered based on the many photographs taken of them.

UPLAND RENDERING TECHNIQUES

Fallingwater is set within a forest of trees replete with undergrowth, tree branches, dead leaves, and moss. The upland portion of the site as well as the area surrounding the house has a brown, textured ground cover composed of dead leaves, with a secondary layer of rhododendron, moss, and small boulders. Sometimes the ground surface is the top of a large rock, with moss and small-scale vegetation along its edge. Of course, there

are various caliper trees throughout the site and numerous young trees at a tertiary level of growth.

The upland portions of the model received a light wash of brown tempera as a base color. Successive layers of texture and rendering mediums were used to establish the ground cover. An effective modeling material used for dirt was masonite. By cutting masonite on a table saw, the dust that remains can be gathered and used as an earth medium by spreading it over an adhesive such as diluted white glue. Also, hobby shops sell a material called "earth", which is a varied texture material that was spread over the masonite "dirt." By gathering actual fall foliage from the ground and placing it in a blender, an additional fine-textured ground cover was similarly spread over the model's base surface. Flocking, very fine rayon fibers, was used to create grass and moss surfaces. It was pumped onto a prepared area of the model with a flocking gun.

An adhesive, either in the form of spray-on rubber cement or green enamel paint, was used to capture the flocking. When the adhesive dried, the excess flocking could be brushed off and reused.

Flocking colors can be mixed. To create a grass color, green and yellow flocking are placed in a bottle. By shaking the two colors, a new color is created by the optical illusion of having a green rayon fiber next to a yellow rayon fiber. The fibers are so small that the wavelengths of light from each fiber appear to mix and become a new color. It is very similar to the dot matrix of a magazine photo. Colors are formed by the juxtaposition of various dots of color.

As the levels of ground cover were built up, additional details, such as rhododendron and small plantings of dried flowers, were added. Dead branches were also strewn throughout the site as well as assorted sized rocks and pebbles. The total finished product, including gravel on the road behind the house, replicated the look and feel of the ground surrounding the house.

THE RHODODENDRONS

An important part of the ground cover was the rhodo-dendrons. The rhododendrons were specific to the Fallingwater site and therefore a generic type of ground cover could not be used for the Fallingwater model. It was necessary to develop a technique that would replicate the rhododendron plantings in a con-vincing manner. Since they are evergreens, a seasonal excuse could not be used to omit them. The rhodo-dendron bush is composed of a whorl of leaves at dif-ferent locations along its branches. The leaves are oblong in shape and pointed at the ends. They often resemble the blades of a propeller. They also are either horizontal or bent upwards or downwards. The model rhododendrons were built of metal. The branches were formed from a series of very thin copper wires twisted together that created the slender trunk, and then untwisted in a series of bifurcations to make additional branchings. The rhododendron whorl in the MoMA model was made of thin aluminum, which was stamped from a sheet by a metal die. In effect, the die punched out an entire whorl of leaves. Of course, the thin metal sheet was prepainted a dark green on the topside and a light green on the underside. After hun-dreds of whorls were punched out, a tiny hole in the center allowed the whorl to be slipped over the cop-per wire of each branching. The branches were already painted a brown color, and as each whorl was put in position, a dab of glue would hold it in place.

When the glue had set, the trunk could be insert-ed through the ground cover and into the foam of the base. The bush was then bent and shaped and the indi-vidual leaves were bent and shaped as necessary, to achieve a natural look.

The rhododendron whorl of leaves for the Monaghan model was made from brass sheets using a photoengraving technique. A photoengraving process etched the whorl of leaves as well as a center hole from a sheet of brass. This sheet was also painted a dark shade of green on one side and a lighter shade on the underside. Multiple rows of whorls were produced on each sheet. The technique proved easier and faster than using an individual punch die.

THE TREES

Another important aspect of the landscaping was the trees. Due to the scale of the model, any technique for making the trees had to be as realistic as possible. Since the season represented by the model is spring just before foliation, many of the trees were spared the need for leaves. Springtime allowed the grass to be green and the waterfall to be at its maximum flow from the winter thaw. The lack of leaves also enabled the house to be more visible.

The trees for the Fallingwater model were actually designed. Each trunk was a carefully selected real tree branch, about 1/2 to 3/4 inches in diameter and relatively straight. The various branchings from this trunk were inserted at an angle into the trunk and then a white plaster was used to blend the joint so it appeared more natural. The process of adding successive smaller branchings along each part of the tree continued until the very last branches, which were quite small.

In order to achieve this very fine network of branches, baby's breath was used. Baby's breath is a dried flower that can be purchased at any florist. Once the small buds at the ends are removed, the remaining branchings resemble the outermost portions of a mature tree. Designing and building each tree was very time consuming, but the results were spectacular.

The next step was painting. The trees were all given a base color of gray lacquer primer. By using an airbrush it was possible to assure painting of each side of every branch. Next, a light brown color was applied from the base of the trunk and blended to the gray of the very last branches. The end branches were left gray in color. The effect of bark was achieved by a "spatter" technique of various shades of brown, dark gray and black paint. This was done using commercial spray cans of paint. Spraying in the air and allowing the particles of paint to settle onto the

OPPOSITE PAGE: **All of the model trees had to be "designed" with successive smaller branchings to achieve a realistic effect. The trees intertwined at the upper levels of the branches.** ABOVE: **View of Monaghan model with internal lighting.**

tree insured that the internal branches received the same effect, as well as the trunk.

When all the trees were completed in various heights and trunk calipers, they were each inserted by size at locations specified by the survey. Each tree was inserted into the foam base and secured by white glue. The area at the base of the trunk was filled and rerendered in ground cover. Since many trees were close together, the upper branches of each tree were often entwined together and had to be carefully positioned to avoid breaking the upper branches.

FINISHING THE BASE

The sides of the base were covered in 3/16-inch-thick acrylic sheets, whose top edges were cut to fit the shape of the topography. These sheets were glued to the plywood substructure as well as to the foam. After each corner was sanded and filled a coat of primer paint was applied. I had long ago established at MoMA, a color for the sides of the bases of models built for them. This gray-brown paint was a latex applied by paint roller. The roller imparted a slight texture to the surface. There was a practical reason for this. Often, the sides of a model are damaged or scuffed and need to be repainted. Using a roller-applied latex paint meant that anyone could repaint a model's base prior to exhibition, thus assuring a clean fresh look to the model.

10

ASSEMBLY

PUTTING THE PUZZLE TOGETHER

HIDDEN SCREW METHODS

As explained in earlier chapters, each floor of the model was not only interlocked together, but also fastened by screws hidden in various places. The very lowest level, or cellar of the house model was screwed into the plywood substructure by screws from below. An 8-32 or 10-32 machine screw was used for all fastenings. A hole was drilled into the acrylic base of the floor and an appropriate-sized tap was used for the machine screws. The Fallingwater model could literally be turned upside down and it would remain intact. The bridge and retaining walls were also screwed from below. The bridge was inserted into the retaining walls from above and a screw inside each corner planter secured it to the wall.

View of the model looking west.

ABOVE: View of the complete north facade with the trellises spanning across the roadway. LEFT: View of the west terrace and base of the model prior to insertion into the landscape. OPPOSITE PAGE: Interior view at the second floor level of wiring and lighting used in the Monaghan model.

EXPANSION JOINTS

The use of acrylic or plastic as the basis for the construction of this model means that it is subject to some expansion or contraction due to temperature changes. Fortunately, museum settings are temperature controlled. But the conditions in my shop meant that there were seasonal differences in temperature, not severe, but enough that sometimes screw holes did not align exactly. To allow for this possibility the hole the screw went through was always slightly larger than the diameter of the screw. This would allow marginal movement in the acrylic. Also, the screw was not tightened but was simply snug, usually with a washer and occasionally a lock washer.

It has also been previously explained that the base of the waterfall is not fastened or glued to the lower stream. This allows some movement for the stream and avoids separation at the shoreline. The rigid styrofoam is minimally affected by temperature changes, even less than urethane foam. The plywood base was also glued and screwed at its joints, which also minimized any potential for movement. Why are these precautions so important? Because understanding and respecting the materials used in the model assured that it would probably need very little repair or maintenance during its lifetime. While expansion joints are not necessarily obvious or even visible, they are nevertheless there and I have no doubt that the Fallingwater model is moving in much the same way as the actual house.

EPILOGUE

When I began model making, I learned a very important lesson while constructing a jewel-like model of a house designed by John Hejduk. When this model was completed it reached a state of near perfection, except for a scratch on the surface of a curved piece of plastic representing a window. I decided to buff that scratch and insure a perfect finished surface. The model had been troublesome to build: tapering airplane-winged cantilevered floors, curved glass surfaces, and a long ramp with accompanying finely detailed railings. Instead of hand buffing the scratch, I took the entire model in hand and applied the scratch to a buffing wheel. To my utter surprise and shock, the buffing wheel caught an edge of the model and hurled it against the concrete wall, breaking it into many pieces. My daughter Selena, who was about four years old, asked what had happened and I motioned her to go away; I was waiting for the blood to return to my brain. I slowly and deliberately repaired and reassembled the model. It never did go back together as well as before, and from that moment forward I resolved that nothing can be perfect. Every model I would build thereafter had a joint or something unfinished that was purposely left that way so that I would not have the opportunity to make it worse. The Fallingwater model has such an unfinished aspect: a joint, purposely unfilled and quite obvious.

The model is distinguished in another way. I collected pieces of broken stone from the site in order to arrive at a stone color.

One of these pieces intrigued me because it looked like a perfectly scaled boulder for the model. I decided to place this piece of stone somewhere in the landscape to represent a piece of the actual house; perhaps it could be the soul of the model. That stone is embedded in the site.

There is a true story I have told many friends about concerning one of the occasions that Arthur Drexler visited my shop to see the model in progress. He was a very observant person. He noticed that there was a droop in the second floor terrace as it cantilevered over the living room. He asked if I could correct this droop; after all, models are perfect. When he left, I delaminated this section and attempted to reglue it with a prestress in the upward direction. Unfortunately, it did not work, the plastic was stretched to its limits and behaved much like the actual concrete. The droop remained. If you visit the house, you can observe this droop from the inside of the living room, sagging as much as one inch. In fact, the window frames are cut to fit within this opening. When I measured the droop in the model it sagged exactly one inch in scale. I also had to cut the windows to fit into the opening.

As if I had not endured enough pain in building this model, which took two years, I was asked to build a second one. In 1987, I was approached by Tom Monaghan, the founder of Dominos Pizza, to construct a model of Fallingwater for his museum in Ann Arbor, Michigan. I reluctantly accepted, and began another two-year project to replicate the model built for MoMA. The Monaghan model had one important extra: It was internally lighted with tiny bulbs situated to duplicate the indirect lighting of the actual house. This was my extra for two reasons. The first model was completely detailed inside, yet not visible once the model was assembled; secondly, I was a little late in delivery so the lighting became an added bonus. It does add another dimension to the model, and although I initially suggested this to Arthur Drexler at MoMA, he did not want it. But the MoMA model is completely detailed and painted on the inside as well.

Model making is a process, and every day a different and better way to make something is discovered. What is important is the discipline and logic applied in solving each problem. Every individual will find his or her way to arrive at a solution. There is no doubt that today there are new materials and better and faster ways to build this model or any other model. I hope that this book has inspired you to think about that process.